WHAT THIS EARTH COST US

This edition first published in 2008 by
The Dedalus Press
13 Moyclare Road
Baldoyle
Dublin 13
Ireland

www.dedaluspress.com

ISBN 978 1 904556 94 7 (bound)
ISBN 978 1 904556 93 0 (paper)

Dedalus Press titles are represented in North America
by Syracuse University Press, Inc., 621 Skytop Road,
Suite 110, Syracuse, New York 13244, and in the UK by
Central Books, 99 Wallis Road, London E9 5LN

Typesetting and design: Pat Boran
Cover image © Elena Ray

The Dedalus Press receives financial assistance from
An Chomhairle Ealaíon / The Arts Council, Ireland

WHAT THIS EARTH COST US

Theo Dorgan

DEDALUS PRESS
DUBLIN, IRELAND

Contents

ROSA MUNDI

WHAT THIS EARTH COST US

Author's Note

This book brings together in one volume my first two collections, *The Ordinary House of Love* and *Rosa Mundi.* Both were published by Salmon Publishing, and I am grateful to the press, in particular to Jessie Lendennie, for that. Each book went out of print quickly, and while *The Ordinary House of Love* had a second printing, thanks to Colin Smythe, it is likely that both might have reached a wider readership given the chance. That, at any rate, is the belief of Dedalus Press and I am grateful to them, in turn, for giving this work a new lease of life.

Every poem is a negotiation between gift and will, or, if you prefer, between the surprise of its unexpected genesis and its process through learned craft to eventual abandonment. Looking back with a cooler, more schooled, eye I found craft errors in some of these poems, a certain unevenness of tone here and there, sometimes a simpler way of saying what I was trying to say. Accordingly, I have taken the opportunity to excise some few poems, to tighten up others. A poem is neither object nor property, it is better perhaps to think of a poem as a moment saved from an unending process. If I found what seems to me now a better way of making a particular poem, I took it; in the main, however, I am happy to let them stand as they first found their way out into the world.

Theo Dorgan
Dublin, 2008

The Ordinary House of Love

to the memory
of my Father and my Mother

For there is no sea
it is all a dream
there is no sea
except in the tangle
of our minds;
the wine dark
sea of history
on which we all turn
turn and thresh
    and disappear

— John Montague

Night Over the Mountain and the City

No rage in the hawthorns or in the State plantations,
only the rain uneasy over Musheramore.
No tumbling of stone in mountain torrents,
only the granite crumbling in the heather.
Here where she laughed in the face of the wind
not a rabbit darts, not a cloud rolls along the ridge.

The lights on the barrack square are shrouded,
and the sentries at whose innocence we guessed
are long gone from the nights of forgotten winter.
Now a car echoing in the empty street awakes no start,
here where she'd toss her hair and wave up to the window,
as in so many places over the years, over the city.

So often in need of soothing, now she is soothed
away forever into a long, untroubled sleep.
So often the ice-breaker on Christmas morning
on swims I could never dare, now she is swimming
out into the dark, as briskly as she strode
over the mountains—leaving us dumb to say

how much we loved her, each in our own way.
How a clear voice echoing in the street will turn our heads,
how a stone crumbling, or a stream rolling or a wave
breaking, will speak of her to us forever.
Too many deaths have unmade my courage for anything
but these images I hold stubborn and unshakable in my heart.

i.m. Clare Barker

Closed Circuit

The light of evening falls in swathes
over the Northside and Blackpool.
Children are rolling downhill
in the long grasses of Bell's Field,
over and over, elbows tucked tight,
drenched in the smell of earth.
They never seem to hit rocks, or roll
in the signature of the city,
broken glass.

Laughter and light trip memory inward,
rooftops press forward
some long-forgotten summer and I fall
in delicious vertigo into a classroom
where I sit silent, staring ...
Even that youngest swallow, climbing
on leafsmoke, starting on the miraculous
journey south, bends downwind for home
though he has never been there.

... I sat in the smell of wood and chalkdust
baked in the sun with smell of the slaughterhouse,
my mind soaring through the roof, neckhairs bristling.
I hung for hours over familiar lanes and streets,
picturing another home in another country.
The call of my classmates after school
were high, wide and shrill—familiar and alien,
the memory neither fades nor fails to haunt—
afternoon music over North African streets.

And today I think you are a village in those mountains.
There are squares and fountains, wells of cool darkness
in the centre of each house, the walls soaked
in a whiteness that makes the heart ache; every house
is a house of mystery, even the scrubbed tables are blessed
with the imprint of your daily use and habit.
Open the drab green shutters and lean out,
I have been flying to you since childhood, and I thirst
for the shock of your fountains, the cool shade of your care;
let me roll like a child forever in your hair.

A Nocturne for Blackpool

Dolphins are coursing in the blue air outside the window
and the sparking stars are oxygen, bubbling to the moon.
At the end of the terrace, unicorns scuff asphalt,
one with her neck stretched on the cool roof of a car.

A key rasps in the latch, milk bottles click on a sill,
a truck heading for Mallow roars, changing gear on a hill.
The electric hum of the brewery whines, then drops in pitch—
ground bass for the nocturne of Blackpool.

The ghost of Inspector Swanzy creeps down Hardwick Street,
MacCurtain turns down the counterpane of a bed he'll never sleep in,
unquiet murmurs scold from the blue-slate rooftops
the Death Squad no one had thought to guard against.

The young sunburned hurlers flex in their beds, dreaming of glory,
great deeds on the playing fields, half-days from school,
while their slightly older sisters dream of men and pain,
an equation to be puzzled out again and again.

Walloo Dullea, homeward bound on the Commons Road, belts
          out airs from *Trovatore*,
the recipe as before, nobody stirs from sleep
and 'Puzzle the Judge', contented, pokes at ashes—
"There's many a lawyer here today could learn from this man".

North Chapel, The Assumption, Farranferris and Blackpool,
the mass of the church in stone rears like rock from the sea
but the interlaced lanes flick with submarine life
older than priests can, or want to, understand.

This woman believed Jack Lynch stood next to God, who broke
    the Republic.
This man beyond, his face turned to the wall, stares at his friend
whose face will not cease from burning in the icy sea—torpedoed off
Murmansk from a tanker. He shot him, now nightly he watches
    him sink.

Here is a woman the wrong side of forty, sightless in her kitchen
as she struggles to make sense of the redundancy notice,
of her boorish son, just home, four years on the dole, foul-mouthed,
of her husband, who has aged ten years in as many days.

The bells of Shandon jolt like electricity through lovers
in a cold-water flat beneath the attic of a house in Hatton's Alley,
the ghost of Frank O'Connor smiles on Fever Hospital Steps
as Mon boys go by, arguing about first pints of stout and Che
    Guevara.

The unicorns of legend are the donkeys of childhood, nobody
knows that better than we know it ourselves, but we know also that
dolphins are coursing through the blue air outside our windows
and the sparking stars are oxygen, bubbling to the moon.

We are who we are and what we do. We study indifference in a
    hard school
and in a hard time, but we keep the skill to make legend of the
    ordinary.
We keep an eye on the slow clock of history in Blackpool—
Jesus himself, as they say around here, was born in a stable.

for Mick Hannigan

Swimming Down Deep to Before Time Began

The night I sank into your troubled eyes
I was watching my words,
I was watching my step
while you were swimming deep into my heart,
gently, disturbing nothing
as the soft rain hung fringes on the trees.

What depths we can sometimes reach,
in unremarkable talk,
in an ordinary caress
sounding truths laid deeper than we know,
gently, disturbing nothing
like people who have been talking for centuries.

If I close my eyes I can feel my breath
as the pain eases out,
as the words ease out,
hesitant, night-swimming fish;
gently, disturbing nothing,
sentences schooling to an unexpected thought:

in Lake Baikal there are boneless fish,
they melt in the shallows,
they melt in the air.
What lives they must lead there in the dark,
gently, disturbing nothing,
lives at an unexpected depth, like ours tonight.

The Mothers, The Children, The Lovers

Our Lady of Flowers is gone from
your city and mine
The children stare vacant, the
grip of their laughter is grim
The soot falls on streets where
you skipped in a loop of strong rope
There's a road through the gardens
where once I robbed apples at night.

The bones of St. Valentine rest
behind Whitefriars walls
And old love is bleeding to death
where we once placed our trust
The trick is to dance beyond
hopelessness and beyond hope
Your eyes on the inward dance
where you may think to find me.

The bellnotes from Shandon fall
silver and cold on Blackpool
And the ladies of Fatima pray
for their thin laughing kids
When I turn in your arms I can feel
the blue lightning start up
The redemption of childhood
the sword held aloft with the cup.

Somewhere your mother and mine
are just starting to talk
In orchards they dreamed of
when young and it wasn't too late

for the vision they had of the love
that flares out in the dark,
in the spell they invoke for us
knowing that our nerve can hold out.

for Paula Meehan

Fledgling

Ungainly biped
by a lurch in time
tipped from the nest

blinks the harsh light
from tender eyes and
stumbles in long grass.

The green blades
are piercing screams.
Massed trees lean over him
with a soft, terrible roaring.

His burgeoning wings mimic
the torsion of drowning
and under this panic
a dreamflash, seen in the egg—
promise of owldark,
a moon fitfully glimpsed
behind bare trees—
and this abruptly extinguished.

Journey By Night

On the high road through the Gorges du Tarn
when the car bucked at a flat turn
and bowled at the edge
on a wedge of rubber screaming,
even then, with the gates of panic breached
we did not break our silence of hours,
our deep trust in the willed path.

And if I now say the depth of time had touched us,
the sense of the great bowl we run down in a curve,
it is only to say what as a child I knew
—there is nowhere to fall
and speed can buttress will —
when you have somewhere to go you simply go.

One Morning in May

The grasses you walk in
are freighted with dew,
your coat flecked
with prismatic drops,
the crystalline rout
of multiplied suns &
the song of the lark
are focused in you

who should be crowned
with flowers and ivy,
your high breasts bare
long hair cascading
over your shoulders—

but what would the neighbours say
to your bright ankles glinting,
to the rippling of the reed-pipe,
to my faun's grin as I perch on the step
of a battered Renault 4?

Sunday Afternoon

In the ordinary house of love
we move quietly from room to room.
Here you are pensive at a window,

your cheek flat on the green pane,
and the oak outside marks
a corner of silence in a summer room.

Beyond again, in a greater room,
swallows curl to a punctured ceiling,
and beyond again …

all of my windows open to the fresh wind,
to the gold light refined through your hair.
A knock on the door of childhood

and the walls dissolve in music,
soft beat of your dancer's foot,
white recession of doorways in your eye.

Next Morning

Starting the engine you smile briefly,
at a button's touch blossom is wiped
to the corners of the windscreen,
crushed fans that stubbornly endure
to my front gate.

Crush me a fistful for token of last night,
white petals drifting at the window,
your breast nuzzling to my lips;
you downshift to move away, avert
your gaze. That's that, then, is it?

Robbing Orchards

I love the parish of the lovers' bed
where the turned-down corners of a sheet,
as I step into a room at evening,
tug at the memory like a half-forgotten street.

The hemmed edge lies at the foot of a wall
I might have climbed, belly warm with danger,
before dropping to the rich, wet grass,
eyes glinting for the laden tree.

Savage delight then, to race dogs to the wall,
scrambling by intuition to the top again
before dropping to the warm pavement, grass stains
on my running-shoes, an apple rolling towards the kerb.

Sometimes you bite me as we fall over the wall
and afterwards I taste apple on my breath,
absolute self in the sweat rolling off my chest,
soaking forever the linen of a remembered street.

Four A.M. Jazz on the Radio

Somebody cynical out there in the dark
brushing the snare with a flick on the backbeat,
midrange piano liquid and blue and the sax
curling under, low; thinking of you.

There's a Forties feel to this,
latenight streets and a single car
far off in the distance, maybe rain
sulky and cool somewhere close by.

Somebody moody is plucking a double bass
like he was drumming on heartstrings,
in the wings, almost, a laidback angel
popping the congas like he was slapping down hope.

Somebody wake that man on the sax,
something a little up-tempo is called for here,
something to get a little focus going
before I light another cigarette.

Radio starlight in the early hours
far from your bed and eyes.
Tell me, the piano man is asking,
how did a kid like you get to be so wise?

A Sudden Grasp of Modigliani

Pungent dust beneath the umbrella pines,
the oily sea licking the smooth rocks.
More than a summer thunder in the air
pressing our conversation down to silence.

And so we walk, together and apart
untouched into the troubled afternoon,
your rope-soled shoes a vivid aquamarine,
scuffing the red dust as we talk of art

and children and the flowers of Provence,
anything but the questions that hang fire
in the yellow clouds pressing from overhead.
The pines are dry as if already dead.

Like a thin thread of water underground
urgently twitching, that the clouds should unburden
and let fall weight of salvation and grace,
my pulse goes through my breathing, snagging yours

until a new rhythm slows time and our walk.
Your eyes are heavy-lidded when I turn to look
and a stray lock follows your cheekbone forward.
Resolution in mid-stride, an end to talk.

"But This Is Most Irregular ..."

In Pushkin's house on the Arbat we put on felt slippers,
to glide between two tours on a private visit.
We are here and not here, and the guides are at first
uneasy. They hand us from room to room, like ambassadors
or prisoners. I admire the tiled walls behind the stove,
the polished floors, the ceilings plain and low.

Portraits and first editions, pages of manuscript behind
glass. Ornaments, polished windows, the poet's writing desk.
There are people before us, we hear their voices; others
behind, heard but unseen. The guides ask urgent questions
of my interpreter, casting me anxious glances, ill at ease.
I feel like the man himself, being processed towards the Tsar.

In primary school we had parquet floors like these; every
Christmas we'd fit socks over our shoes and glide in lines
from end to end in glorious misrule until the floors shone
like polished apples. The impulse is irresistible—I start
skating around John Field's old black piano and in a sudden
crack of sun everything comes right. The guide's face

breaks in a smile and she sheds her careworn years, Lena
is grinning from ear to ear and another guide appears and then
we are all four revolving in a slow ring, mayhem and
giddiness in the poet's house at last. A horseman riding by
would find us hard to resist, would surely refuse his destiny.
To be cast in bronze forever could never compare with this.

The House on the Edge of Silence

Come and lie long beside me one more time,
long and slender beside me through this quiet night,
beyond passion or the body's ambition, merely tender
and cool, listening to the silence between heartbeats.

We'll have sheets of starched white linen
and heavy blankets to press us under
the surface into quiet deeper than sleep.
We'll have the blue October light
and keep each other awake with minute shifts in place,
contact withdrawn at the ankle, renewed at the hip.

Tonight for the last time we'll let the moorings slip,
pushing our lovers' boat away from the stone house
under the elms, pushing them out into the lake
of forgotten dreams, pushing them out and away
from us as they turn to each other under the stars with
a practiced and complete ease, so sure of themselves ...

We'll have rest then that we never dreamed of
that first time and the many times since when
we slowly undressed in this room, hearing the silence deepen.
We'll have rest as we watch them drift out into the dark,
marking each wave-slap against wood with a caress,
twining themselves in the rhythm of what is.

Bright stars winking in the clear month before winter.
We always knew, even when soaring into that first lift,
it would come on a night like this—the elms creaking
on the margins, lake slapping against stone, timbers settling
to the swell. Bodies reaching to surpass themselves.
An old story, unfolding on the ceiling.

Beyond heartbreak and joy, the silence between heartbeats.
After all our journeying and fret, this promised room.
Come and lie long beside me one more time,
long and slender beside me through this quiet night.

Four Thousand Survivors

The horse of the century trembles
under the alder tipped with bronze,
flanks of black silk raked by thorns.

He has made a long flight in terror,
fleeing the sea of millions dead
to this place of water

beneath tall cliffs, thicket of sun,
swell of birdsong; his shadow creeps east
to his birthplace as evening ignites.

Rearing, his head among branches, he flails
the bright air, churning close turf, nostrils
flung wide to the savour of earth

then plunges to part the green waters;
shouldering out, clattering on submerged rock,
white roar of the waterfall in his ears.

High on the cliffs the assembly lifts to depart.
Young men put on the wings of eagles,
women already are treading air.
A clear bell-note fractures the horizon.

Morning in Winter

Your eyelash rasping on my stubble
we puff breath at the window,
through the clearing pane watch
birds on crisp branches,
the city skyline emerging.

The long garden invites
that we step out,
to feel white grass crunch
underfoot, heel slide over
stalks wet under frost.

Soft shock on the window, snow
funnelling through the tall elms.
We snap into waking
as loops of your laughter
fall ringing on my ears,
we dress and fall out
into a world made over, new.

Wedding Guests on the Anniversary

They vanished in a flare of light and laughter,
the dark doorway torched by her dress and veil.
We could hear them crossing the hushed water-meadow,
the car coughing into life, the roar dwindling.

Now we can hear a different car approach,
ghost of a car's ghost tunnelling up the years,
we strain to the windows to imagine them,
the open door spilling light into the yard.

Time we were gone. We'll leave them to the wine
on the scrubbed deal table, the ticking clock
and all the talk they've gathered from the years.
No fear but they've plenty to look back on

and look forward to. We have other care,
blessed if they grasp at the same luck as this pair.

for Marie and Seamus

Birthday

Red wine in white porcelain bowls,
Susan is having a birthday and
we are all invited.

Bread smells from the yellow kitchen,
broad armfuls of corn, tied with red ribbon,
hang from the rafters, baskets
of fruit range along shelves

and there is music like crystal,
music that strays from the raw hills,
music of many voices, tangled
in easy conversation.

Bushels of flowers are heaped in the windows,
ripe yellow rushes carpet the floor—
gathered by Nuala of the pale shoulders—
each knock brings an old friend in from the door.

Red wine in white porcelain bowls.
Susan is having a birthday and
we are all invited.

Savage

My love is a cat
and has me plagued with
claws and scratches, feline
insouciance and
her habit of dropping
from lamp-posts and branches,
battening on my scruff.

Sometimes she's nice
and brings me roses, dangling
from her slack jaw—
fresh-cut, blood red roses.

Kilmainham, Easter

Blood and cold stone, rust
bleaching to a scurf of crystal,
stain on the jailyard
paving we cannot lift.

Crash of the volley and our hope.
When they carried out your stretcher
the yard darkened to a well of shame
and steadily it grows darker.

This is the shrine our rulers keep
and today they have graced it with flowers.
Let us grant them at least their honesty,
their naked love of prisons.

to the memory of James Connolly

All Souls' Eve

Deirid lucht léinn gur chloíte an galar an grá ...
Nuair a théas sé fá'n chroí cha scaoiltear as é go brách.

Once a year in a troubled sleep
that room stands drenched in light
where I sit and watch us both asleep
in a cold sweat of fright.

A high room where the boards creak
the skylight faced with frost
our bodies interlaced in sleep
and the world long lost.
Beside the bed my blue jeans
lie crumpled in your dress
dawn light coming in as we
unconsciously caress.

The germ of death is in that dream
there in our mingled breath
there in our silence and our speech
—as when you moan *not yet.*
We lie in the breath of lovers lost
to the world since time began
their souls the patterns in the frost
as you turn beneath my hand.

Once a year in a troubled sleep
I watch until we wake
... this is a vigil that I keep
and never must forsake
until slow bells break

from a world long lost
sleep-drugged lovers
to a city gripped in frost.

There is no time and all time
as we surface to a kiss
what we were before we died
a game compared to this.
No world and a whole world
in an innocent caress
never again the same world
we leave when we undress.

> *The learned men say that love*
> *is a killing disease.*
> *When it goes to the heart*
> *it will never come out again.*

Catching the Early Morning Train

Drowsy in perfumed sleep you turn and watch
as I rise in the cold air to dress,
finding my things by touch, in a gleam of streetlight.

Courage is needed to leave, courage to watch.
The gravity we can sometimes hold at bay
is the real power at moments like this.

Isn't it strange?
We shift between what we claim and what claims us,
neither free nor unfree, neither moving nor at rest.

Sharp wind off the river cuts your perfume,
a boat hoots mournfully, standing out to sea.
How hard it is to resume the you and me.

Song: Premonition

Into my mind a ship came sailing,
in her hold you lay as dead,
at your feet white wolves were howling,
seven bright candles were at your head.

On the bare oak deck lay a sheaf of barley,
dolphins plunged in the foaming wake,
high astern hung glinting stormbirds,
curls of ice in the vault of day.

I thought of the mountain on which we rambled
to view the landfall to Kenmare Bay,
I saw with the mind's eye that silver birchwood
where drunk with love we often lay.

In the lane this morning a curl of woodsmoke
called up your face in the winter air,
a dark foreboding was in your features,
a lightning-chaplet restrained your hair.

All the long day great winds are rising,
salt lightning roars rock to shining clay,
a hawk erupts through the rainlashed window,
bright talons gleaming in a burst of spray.

Oh where are you now, where do you lie,
what storm confounds you, homeward bound?
Send me a sign the line's not broken, that
binds your heart to our home ground.

She Invites

When unringed fingers move to weave
she ceases momently to breathe,
an old blues floats in to fill
the space departing dancers leave.

Her eyes flash
from inward focus, hips
barely move, except when
her belly's concave shifts
to trap stray notes.

Spare and select, her gestures
grace the lean music, they pull time
and the lines of the room
to a tight, breathing cage.

Press of the music parts her lips,
heel hammers a slow beat
and she swoops to greet me—
black hair flaring, her arms held wide.

for S.A.

Her Body

Becomes pure power
sufficient to self
a form of light.

Sprayhead she fountains
in whirling of stars
benefactress of galaxies
axis of night, until
brightcrown bows down
and she flares, turning, then
dies to her root in damp earth.

Through slant fields at twilight I am drawn
to learn my nature at her feet.

Song: Black Fox Wood

By Black Fox Wood I came
and stood an hour before your door.
By first light I had forgot
what I was waiting for.

In that wood there is a tree
whose roots plait in a rushing stream.
As I returned again I met you
waiting there for me.

We kissed, and I remembered what
I'd waited for an hour.
When I got to your house again
you were standing in the door.

We kissed, and stood in Black Fox Wood.
Embraced, and then instead
of close turf and the wild thyme
we were sprawled across your bed.

And ever since it's all the one
to me, love, where we are—
under the light of a paling moon
or a dark and wayward star.

The bed became our marriage-bed
and each the other's good
whether here on a city street
or at large in Black Fox Wood.

At the Lubyanka

No queues yesterday, Anna Akhmatova,
at the black ice-bound gates of Kresty Prison.
Tonight a bride in a veil of lace
walks hand in hand with her young man
through grim Dzherzinskaya of eternal shame
without a backward or a sideways glance,
the bell of her laughter antiphon to your *Requiem*.

Now that the terror has changed key,
now that it drifts like ash, like
funeral music through the veins of
the wide world, tell me
where will the grief of mothers find
the point of its pure expression,
where should we hope to find now a voice like yours?

Insomniac

Her long arms encircle,
will never hold me,
whose hair on my pillow

is honey-coloured
even in moonlight,
her sharp features
blurred in sleep.

My friend is untouched
by winter's breath.
Her skin blooms to velvet
soft to the touch.

Her necklace lies in a pool of wine,
it bruised my lips when she
crushed me close, as her words
still bruise my heart:

You who have not learned patience
must first learn care, then
come to trust who grips the knife
that cuts the lifeline to give life.

Floating after making love you are often
oracular. Will it be you curled here beside me,
burrowing your cold nose against my ribs,
who will deliver me to death?

The Sea-Gypsy and Her Lover

He

I am the murmuring surf beneath the nocturne,
the shearwater piercing the wave arcade.
I am the wrist and gesture of the gypsy,
I am the wavearch and her figure in the arch,
I am the hair falling across her face
and the clear stars drizzling through her hair.
My breath is the far-off murmur of the surf
and my true songs are nocturnes.

She

Turning and building back always on my heart
I am the oldest port you ever sailed for,
mine in the dog-watch is the unseen hand
that pulls the helm over into the belly of a wave,
mine and mine only the brief skyward path
climbing the silver inside of the uproll when the moon spins
and the heart calls inward *home, home*—

I am the music then,
I am the clash of bracelets and the space hung
where the seabird was,
mindless and cold like the long roar of the surf,
nailed for all time to the crossmast of your bones.

Eye of the Storm

i)

Drumrolls on the windowpane,
forked lightning over the terraced
city where I find myself again.

ii)

High in your room we float, caught
up in play of star and planet,
feeling the pulse of common orbit.

iii)

Each cell of me swells
to your lunar pull,
we rise up
and overflow
the well-walled earth.

iv)

Limitless, the lid-pictures
of selves beyond skin

Silence beyond the bloodveil
hiss in the ear fading

rain coming downhill among trees

Revenant

Pale gleam of her hips
as she swings by.
Black fall of her hair
brushes her shadow on the wall.

smell of woodsmoke as I rise and follow

Alder taps on the windowpane,
leafshadow flickering
on a harpsichord.
Fingers of ivory drift

out over the black keys
as she hunches to begin.
But instead she turns,
unhoods her eyes for me.

smell of jasmine, nettles, earth after summer rain.

for P. McS.

Coming Events

Consider the ghostlines feeding the piper,
his face draining to mask of stone,
the liquid death in his music; look

how he coaxes a last grace from the space
between stars, how his wrists battle the chanter ...
Now set your foot to the green lament.
We are but shadows fixed in flesh,
this earth a greeting-place.

The Archer's Toxin

You are more vulnerable than you were,
loving me more than you did before
love's bite struck bone.

Fragility is strength, we know the paradox.
The question in your eyes, which mirrors mine, is
what, when we walked here first and had not
certainty of love, made both hearts beat one beat?

In the Metro, Moscow

No buskers at the gate,
the only time I have ever gone
underground without music.
No advertisements on the wall,
nothing to speak of the world,
to tempt us back.
Bronze of Pushkin, polished
and serene; in the overhead frieze
planes of the Thirties,
a parachutist descending.

The first stage is easy
but at the interchange
I hesitate, spelling
the letters of an unfamiliar tongue.
A woman my mother's age approaches,
examines the card on which I have
carefully written down my destination.
Gripping my elbow she sets off
through the labyrinth. I tell her
my nation; she is indifferent, amused.

I am borne along under warm arrest.
We cross corridors, climb stairs,
descend again, turn corners,
eventually we arrive. Meanwhile
her daughter is embarrassed, furious.
I shake hands with the mother but
I am looking at the daughter.
Her face is a mask of insolent stone,
clamped in stereo headphones.
I wonder what journey I have interrupted.

Almost

Stooping at night to shield a match
from the street wind, or stopping
to watch the dust lift from
the cracks between paving stones,
I see your feet pick crisp steps into the afternoon,
a small pain twisted into your shoulders.

A moment neither accepted nor refused.
Though the match flares and goes out,
though the dust hangs in my eye,
I remain hunched, trapped in the dream
of your small feet walking away,
the look in your eye before you turned.

for Thomas and Catherine

Falling South

It might be a prairie scene from the American Midwest:
a ruined farmhouse in a dry, ploughed field, the melancholy
burned out of it by the high Beltane sun
The outlandish voices around me falling silent.

Rocked on the morning train I gather images,
select, discard, the eye seduced by what's thrown up
at random, the ear tuned to Dido's last great aria
How the thing surfaces from what is random.

It might be a wood I plunged in as a child after school,
released to the mysteries of the grove by an act of will,
this copse spinning quickly from the corner of vision
The world might be random, selection never is.

The day comes when the heart tires of duty and care,
tires of the endless effort to hold to the mooring chain,
and the mind invests its ambition in the senses
Sun on my hand, the deserted farmhouse, trees in their stillness.

In every trip that I make there is a voice speaking,
I drift in my seat, straining to catch the wavelength,
to grasp something coherent in the space between cities
But it falls away in a reverie of your highflown hands.

The sun drifts high against lichened cottage walls,
I imagine the silence we might make there before night
comes in, but I cannot imagine this as a promised life
Falling away to the south in a sensual freefall.

Atavist

I am a flame crossing the river
rain is hissing on the water
I do not waver but incline
against the vector of my passage
fin of some great seagoing fish.

And though this bridge
husband its carriageway
to a ribbed vaulting aisle
I am crossing a whale-road
under arch of bleached bone,

the flame that I am
on this dark night at your window
burned before Christ.

Statement of the Political Exiles

If it takes anger, we will be angry.
If it takes patience, we will be rock
stubborn in the stream.
If it means forced marches
in the dead of the night,
look for us when the moon is down,
one foot steady after the other.

If it means prison,
bind our wrists, take us.
If it means beatings
we will break like reeds,
like reeds we will spring back
after the storm has gone over.

We can be silent in the airports,
our songs locked in our hearts.
We can be faceless
in your cities,
anonymous in your fields;
we can dissolve like salt
in the sea of tears,
we can be sand
drifting at the margins.

If it takes all the aeons needed
to crush carbon into diamond,
hear us:
those rivers run in our blood,
that garden was promised us
before time began.

Who owns the light?
Who has charge of the air?
If it takes anger
we will be angry but
in any case, believe us:
we are surely going home.
Can you make a bird
fly backwards?
Believe us, we are going to our home.

for Kader & Louise Asmal

Dr. Hoffman's Discovery

The lichen blooms
into light and strikes,
curled edges already
beyond the forehead,
skirmishing inward
to the brain's light.

The brain's light,
determined
to sell itself dearly.

On a day in summer over Ballingeary
walking the hills with nothing in mind
I stopped too long by a glowing rock
and lost my reason to the god of war.

A stone will do it,
a drop of water
at a leaf's tip,
will trip your defence
and feed you to the world.

Mars is a sponge for light,
a god of harvest;
in the brute swing of his arc
your light has perfect value, perfect weight.

Woman in Forest

I imagine you rising from a dark pool
late sun, early moon silvering your black hair.
A still pool, and the forest musk
rank in the ferndust where I lie.

Late evening, then, when all the creatures
are watchful and at rest,
You reach for your cheekbone with your palm,
considering the reflection of yourself.

All my attention's on the slow fall
of water through your hair; your eyes
are agates there, I'll rue the day
they fix on me in judgement.

Meanwhile, like any fox or rabbit,
I drink in the evening air,
lap at your waist as you rise up,
gambling with my whole future in your stare.

Day of Reckoning

i)
Harpnotes like motes in the clear air
skylight tipped high to morning

Sunlight in bars on your tawny flank
soft cheek muting the strings

How many nights under sheets of lead
for this plangent, parting air?

ii)
Framed in a blue door you mouth bubbles of gold
and your hand bobs in an underwater salute

My ear is a tall sail
tilting toward your blessing

Time boils in my veins
I shrug and displace myself.

iii)
In the full glare of noon
white waves on a white beach

Swallows in panic stitching the wound
seathistles leaching to acid green

Sweat starts to my bleached palms
dull presentiment pounds in the blood.

iv)
Climb inland. Far beneath, a deep pool—
and down dives an arrow-arc of water

Blue translucent deer
ricochet off the wall of my look

My love is a drowned white city,
submarine light gilding her towers.

v)
Quartz leaps from the hammer blow
in the waning light

Repetitive echoes map valleys of dusk
a heron fades down the river's fall

A worker is quarrying stars
shards fountaining in his face.

vi)
On the high plantation road
a fox comes careless of noise

A wheel coming up through bracken
a fox careless of noise

We stitch the wound with a look
silent regarding silent.

vii)
The wind stirs in the pinetops and
the dark is climbing towards me from the sea.
Here I pick up my solitary way.

Starring the gulf between us,
the cottage lights flick on.
I cannot tell which of them now is yours.

> *Star of the valleys,*
> *star of earth,*
> *star that was counted*
> *and is now lost.*

Carnival

Sing carnival when the mind freezes
then turns on its own meat, carnival
before the long fast, carnival that we turn
to drink at the blood wells of memory.

Savage simplicity, in the bleached palms
of the self-regarding dancers;
savage and clear, the energy
of the self-disclosing dancers.

The flare of a star multiplies
in the Easter sky; each blade
in the clearing is hammered to its shadow.
There is a dipping ring of torches
and dancers counter-revolving in a ring.
There is a roaring fire at the heart,
the flames wailing over the mad earth
flailing hosannas to the coming Beast.

Sing carnival indeed, a feast of man—
you who love language and light, sing while you can.

Nora Harkin Remembers Peadar O'Donnell

A man in a red shirt
Can neither hide nor retreat
—Hugh MacDiarmid

The shutters have closed forever on the big windows.
You'll look no more on street nor heaving field
and the sea will have your spirit, the ungovernable sea
that rolls against Bloody Foreland, rolls against Ireland.

It would be like you, when the gate flies open, to duck home
on a flying visit, on the run even from death,
to breathe for a last time air of Tír Chonaill,
before facing seaward, to the next job to be done.

> *I like to think of their indomitable forms,*
> *Connolly, Mellows, Gilmore, Davitt, Tone,*
> *standing like stars on the waves, savouring the joke*
> *that indeed they live forever, as you will live forever.*

Perhaps a fisherman far out from home will see the light—
a deckhand out of Burtonport, a kinsman—as your stocky form
comes marching out from shore, glowing already in the web
of new life, looking for comrades and for work.

I'll bet you he keeps his mouth shut, sensible man.
He'll turn from the forepeak, stub out the cigarette
and join in the hauling of the heavy net. His is a world of work
like yours, a world of sober fact, of bread and basics.

Home with the dawn and turning in the door I see him go
to the big windows, flinging the shutters open to the clear air
before he goes through to wake his wife and daughter,
humming an air thoughtfully, *O'Donnell Abú.*

The Witness

Lorca testing a ragged song
in the café of the sad guitars.
By his feet on the stone floor
an almost-empty bottle, by his hand
a candle, cone of light in dark.
The voice choking on itself and silence.

Chairs on the table; a lone waiter
waters a rich profusion of plants.
Death sits by the door to the street,
eyes closed, tenderly nursing the song.
I am the stranger buried in the shadows,
easing my bones on a hard, wooden bench.

I write on a postcard that nothing has been gained here.
The song will not carry him beyond himself,
will not dissolve the sweating walls,
cannot unveil the starry dimensions ...

The waiter inhales the invigorated earth.
The courtly old man opens my door home.

Gaia

She torches to touch us, tortured,
turning slowly on her long axis,
bones kindling to the dry fire.

Betrayed, seared to the quick,
deep in herself she nurtures
a dark spring beneath high breasts.

Who would have chosen to live in these times,
on a planet studded with fire,
the flood welling in her heart that will engulf us?

for John and Evelyn

70

The Father of Holocaust

I father the holocausts like a bull,
I am the yellow flame scouring the womb,
I drink the protein of the bloodflow,
I am the taste of copper and despair.

I am the endless grinding convoys
and the entrails gorged with corpses,
soundlessly bellowing over the endless waves
of entire nations stampeded to the pit.

My fire is your quickening into death.
I have thickened the humus with blood,
sifted your fields with bonemeal,
not a blade of grass but is stained with my work.

Under the grains and orchards,
under the autobahns and railroads,
I am the subsoil of black ash
under the cities and cathedrals of the plain.

Mine are the ovens whose smoke hangs
in the chambers of your mind,
in the Zyklon chambers I am the mind
delighting in its dance of veils

and I am the silence ticking beneath your pulse,
I am the weariness of the daily horror
endlessly repeated, I am the numbness and the silence
after the bombers have gone over.

Mine are the children and the burning homes
mine are the smooth urbanities of Ministers
mine are the fountains of earth flesh and fire
mine are the flowers of napalm in the silence.

    I give you a mirror of your own devising
    that you may see me, the god over your shoulder.

Here are the factories and houses,
here the white hospitals and churches
here the eternal towers of Auschwitz
seen in a glass darkly,

seen in the quiet streets of Dresden
fused in the vortex of my fire,
the sign you have raised across the living earth,
your blood tribute to my lust and care.

    I give you a mirror of your own devising
    that you may study me, the god over your shoulder.

Lear Garlanded with Age

Nothing will come of nothing—
the king dripped spittle into
a widening, an appalled silence.
The feathered reptile flashed in the dark,
fledged in the old man's gut.

Oh he was fastidious in his exile,
his bowels churning, his head in a fever,
mad in his journeying yet cleaner in this
than his crushed and cold companions.

What cracked him open to the wind's work?
His daughter's exile was cliff without shelter.
Here he held court with himself, crying to God
for a straw of meaning, relief from the upland wind.
The Fool and the Blind Man guarded him there.

From where but from death in life, from
where but from nothing should he climb down,
the long grasses around him like his years
to find at the pit's edge, stopped,
his loving, now his lost, Cordelia?

His eyes in their uneven orbits leap
across time, grey bloodsoaked arena,
Eyes of a victim, mute.
An old mudcaked father, half a man,
bringing flowers of ruin to a daughter's triumph.

for Seán Lucy

73

Night Letter

Whether that gnaws at me which long habit
persuades me I daily see, or that which
I sometimes, unbearably, touch
and think I know but fail to name,
dear friend I cannot say.

Night after night I sit here and it gnaws at me,
something undone that cries out to be done;
it is a dilute acid in my blood,
it is the characters of your name
tried on a white sheet here before me.

There is an order I can't touch, it sears me.
There is a hollow in my palm, however hard
I push I cannot flatten it to the table.
There is an endless terror in such fact.
I want the order to protect me.

I want the fact of flat to be my guardian—
I skate above electrons when I walk,
I nest among electrons when I sleep—
there are nights here when the floor is a sheet of glass,
the flat face of a bottomless shaft of darkness.

Tonight again I sweat the memories out:
an old, broken General in the asylum
I drill my talismans across the table,
hoping by perseverance and cold patience
to stumble on order that will stop the rout.

Tomorrow again the descent into the city
down long hills, past old sandstone walls,
past butcher and breadshop, restaurant and bar—
calling each thing familiar as a charm,
hoping to hear the name of what we are.

Long Valley Vignette

In the drained glass,
in the barman's smile as you
slowly grow absent,

as in mirrors that repeat
a childhood nightmare,
no reflection.

You say, we live in Babel.
You say, we live in Hell.
Nobody disagrees.

You stare in the mirror
and childhood is very near,
a thirsted-for oblivion.

Humphrey! Allow me to
buy this man a drink.

for Humphrey and Rita Moynihan

Your Childhood

Today, walking in hard light,
broken, refracted, cascading
over children at play,
I saw as from high over earth
your child's face reflecting the light
from the underside of leaves.

There was dust on your cheek, my dear,
dust on your burning cheek.

Twin

I am a voice in towering stillness
I am the absence of that voice
and the child's coat it trails behind closed doors.
I am the memory you will never have,
incident at the centre of your life.

I am the echo launched both ways at once,
backward into the blue sea and forward
into the arms of living death.
I am that death whose cry ripped out the echo,
mine was the third voice of your conception.

When you first pulsed into a clot of flesh
beating outward to the rosepink light,
I was the living measure of your need.
When the blue mesh built out beneath your skin,
humming with blood and sugars,
I was the chord that sang you into life.

When you began the long, bloody slide
into the lights and airs of this crazed planet
I was the absence you already felt.
I was the echo fading in your wake,
I was the strongest contraction and the push,
the cry beating against you like white light.

I am the voice you search for and forget,
I am its absence for good reason,
better to hunt for than to find.
Look in your father's and your mother's grave—
you die if you find me, die if you do not search.

The Thaw

Moscow 1987

A great dome of frost stands over the taiga,
blue as the dome of the great mosque of Samarkand.
A great dome of absolute, virgin silence
pierced by the bell-like voices of unseasonal birds.

The very sap rising in the birches is frost,
the snow underfoot rings with tiny, clear echoes
as the foot of a man crushes whole cities
of galleried, honeycombed crystal with each step.

Somewhere a simple man is burning logs,
it is mid-morning and time for a cup of tea.
He fancies he hears, dying away through the forest,
the echoes of his axe, notes from a fading bell.

In the honeycomb of his memories, a lone voice is ringing,
tiny and clear and golden, calling the faithful to prayer.
Meanwhile over the immense taiga, Mandelstam is trudging
—towards Voronezh, or Moscow?

Actress

I was the gesture when you crossed yourself,
the tendon tightening when you arched your foot,
the last bar on the violin, your cue; I was
the swell of woodwind when you crossed the bar,
who but I had the set so carefully dressed?

I was the dusty board on which you stood,
the pod of air beneath your arch, the dust
that filmed your calves, the glint of talc;
I was the sweat in beads at tip of eyebrow,
I was the heat of you moving in the hush.

I was the blaze of light in which you walked,
the cool hand that dimmed the ticking spot;
I was the fly-bar and the drop,
your grip as you found the pace,
the cage of breath and gesture that you made.

Where is your lover now that you've stepped out
beyond the daily confines of the self?
The knees that kneel here rested behind his
but the heart, ah the heart stutters to another beat,
the struggle behind your speech the birth

of complicity, a foot set treacherously on a bridge.
I am the pole at either end of the bridge.
Mine are the author's fears and yours,
I the possession you both court and fear.
Have I not laid these heads beneath your feet?

I had the image made that lured them in,
I had the food contrived to tempt you,
I am the food of breath, the breath that feeds you
over the footlights into the cage your compact makes,
I am the darkness when the circuit breaks.

I am the actress and the act,
I am an exquisite gesture and its vanity,
I am the face resumed before the mirror.
I am the unreal street when you step out—
who but I had the set so meticulously dressed?

Song: Elusive

My love she made a net of light
and set it up before my path,
at its heart, as black as night,
a curved salmon sat.

Between the apple and the oak
she stopped me on my morning walk
with such a deft and desperate art
she made me stumble in my talk.

The voice inside me since my birth
curved off into the shining trees,
my new attention perched there too
and wondered what to make of me.

A blackbird in a bead of light
trembled on the nearest leaf
and, from behind, his piercing song
stalked my sudden grief.

A cold wind made the salmon dance
and the same wind brought me down,
from a great height over earth and time
I stood on common ground.

The blackbird spread to the rising wind,
the salmon danced in the net—
although my love cannot be found
she may come to me yet.

Waking

Halfway from sleep.
Attention snags
on a windwave breasting alders,
then whirls away on the pollen spume.

I wake in a valley of braided rivers.
walking through beaded grass.
My whistling loops with the swift
in the smell of broad earth.

Sun ray lances from behind my shoulder,
crashes against your window in a green spray.

Here are pale mushrooms in a basket,
cider and fruit, crisp in the frost,
for our breakfast on the mountain. Step
out and walk with me in the fresh light of day.

Return

I can't see my hand at arm's length
but I see her face, shining with mist & sweat
as the boat dances in to the beach.

Nearly dawn: not long now until feet
slap in the shallows, where water and sand
have an always shifting frontier.

The creak of the oarlocks is louder, nearer—
here come the herring gulls, her escort.

Thermal

Peregrine spiralling
over moorland well,
lower and lower to mate
with his reflection.

Had not the wild rose
burst into flame
he was lost forever
to the high plain.

Speaking to My Father

How should I now call up that man my father,
who year after weary year went off to work,
buried his heart beneath a weight of duty,
buried himself early so that we might live?

How should I sit here and explain to his shade
that, yes, this is the work I do you died for,
this is the use I make of all that sacrifice —
I move the words as you moved heavy tyres.

True, there is no sickening stench of rubber,
no heat from the curing pans, no rage
at management, choked back by need as much as pride—
but father, the range of uselessness is wide.

Often, as I grew slowly, you'd let slip
a word, a helpless gesture or a look
that shook me to the roots. I'd sense the void
you stubbornly, heroically sweated back.

Now I have everything you lacked, above all
freedom to shape the workload for the day—
it sounds like freedom, doesn't it? The truth is,
I hate the shiftwork just as much as you did.

There are days lately, as I thicken in years,
when I feel your sinews shift inside my frame,
I catch a look of yours in the mirror, shaving—
mild, sceptical, weary, a bit resigned,

but something else too: your athlete's way
of planting the feet carefully when troubled,
shoulder square to the blow that may come,
ready and fit to defend what you hold dear.

What troubled you most? The question shies away
when I stab with my pen, clumsy as ever
—I don't even rightly know what troubles me,
ignorant as when I rode upon your knee.

What would you make of me, I wonder, sitting here
long after midnight, searching for the words to
bring you back, soliciting the comfort of your shade
for the odd, useless creature that you made?

Here is the end of all that education,
the void is as close to me as it ever was to you.
I make poems as you and Rose made children,
blindly, because I must.

Father, comrade, the same anger with the world
but not your patience moves me. I make you this,
a toy in words to re-introduce myself
and to ask: what must I do to be your child again?

Rimbaud's Nurse

I am the nurse of the small hours,
crushing phials of morphine with my heel,
I am the oiled linoleum angel,
the rack in my look and the cold bedframe.

In the case of Arthur Rimbaud ...
in the Hospital of the Immaculate Conception
Marseilles 1891,
where his knee burned to bend again
and the crows of Cyprus creaked in his eyes,
where his leg was and was not,
where his wrist burned with an old wound,
a wound of love that was not, neither wound nor love,
over and over I listened to him beg
Let me go to the sea, let me go to the sea.

I was the swarming cancer of his need,
black Venus hull-down on the horizon.

I am the starch and press of night
I am the sweat pressed from nightmare
I am the nurse of the small hours
crushing phials of morphine with my heel.

For pity I reserve a particular silence,
neither memory nor oblivion in my gift.

The Promised Garden

There is a garden where our hearts converse,
at ease beside clear water, dreaming
a whole and perfect future for yourself,
myself, our children and our friends.

And if we must rise and leave,
put on identity and fight,
each day more desperate than the last
and further from our future, that
is no more than honour and respect shown
to all blocked from the garden that we own.

There is a garden at the heart of things,
our oldest memory guards it with her strong will.
Those who by love and work attain there
bathe in her living waters, lift up their hearts and
turn again to share the steep privations of the hill;
they walk in the market but their feet are still.

There is a garden where our hearts converse,
at ease beside clear water, dreaming
a whole and perfect future for yourself,
myself, our children and our friends.

Khayaam Was Right

Khayaam was right, we are toys
on the table of existence but cast
beyond the nursery tale's confines,
you to your unknown future, I to mine.

Prison me in your dreams of what should be,
set me to match a long-prefigured step,
what do you have then if you hold me
but a child's toy to guard in sleep?

Gently, the tales of childhood are no more,
the nursery beams are charred, they stink in the rain,
and we must make new mysteries of our own
before we achieve that innocence again.

Gently, the road behind us falls away,
the walled garden fades into a dream.
Kiss me and touch my cheek, then choose your path:
neither will keep this rendezvous again.

Rosa Mundi

for Paula Meehan

"Even as we freeze in Lethe
we will remember
the seven heavens
this earth cost us"

—Osip Mandelstam

prologue

name on stone
shadow on path
moon behind
latticework of branches
all so deceptively simple
the wind over the crosses
the name on the wind

I had that name
and lived between those dates
printed on paper, carved in stone—
I was the seed and now am clay
this birch more part of me than you are

Thornship

A thornship lifted from the blown hedge,
white rags to carry her head
and a wren her pilot.

High in the blue of March a hawk wheeled
out of the archaic, and a crow's rattle
dragged back along her wake.

I set my heart to follow her lift,
shifting my ground as to the manner born—
borne up and out with her,

the spume of blossom dusting my eyes.
The wind thrummed in her rigging,
the wren dropped back

along her broad track and she dipped for the north,
a fine strain in her ribs, her decking
meticulously fit.

How long she rose and where she carried us,
what we saw from that height, how many
we were, and from where,

doesn't matter now. Dream up alongside,
my salty love of May, settle your feathers
here beside me, fit for the journey.

House Over the Harbour at Ballintoy

Carrick-a-Rede, Port Ballintrae, the Causeway,
a long day spun out in sea and granite. We turn
on a whim into a tight-wound hill and down past
an alien house to Ballintoy.

Not a room in that house where a man or woman could
stretch out, built by an artist to face down the nights:
the view is west to Donegal and the basalt columns
of a fallen city.

Chamber-tombs, passage-graves and double raths, Union
flags and bunting to confuse the French visitor.
Our friends pick flint and herb from the day's flow
to season their lives.

    A disjointed land.

We play at tourists, unhappy and at home
where the road from Tara ends in Dunseverick crumbling
on its rock, and a snug harbour opens
new arms to Scotland.

The eye picks trim pleasure-boats at anchor, children galvanic
where waves foam through a notch in rocks; Greeks would
have tavernas here, lamb from the hill field smoking
on charcoal with Atlantic fish.

But, the times that are in it, the fresh quay walls, the landing stage
tempt a military read: a perfect harbour for landing craft, enough
room to turn a truck. A discreet place to work into if the worst
should come to the worst.

I've read that the Swiss build highways with air force jets in mind,
as Haussmann laid out the boulevards for their lines of fire—
what a species we are for value, the savings recouped in over-
   lapping maps.

As I roved out...

Indeed. I reach my hand up to my love walking the wall, pure
happy. I imagine pushing her face into gravel as the shots ring out,
cowering as heavy boots smack desperately for cover, or the heart-
   stopping silence as

dressing behind rocks we hear the van's engine, the muffled
   outboard
in the darkened bay. I think of the architect Albert Speer.
   The strange house
is a watchtower for times of shallow sleep,
when boats at night make the skin crawl like the sea.

for Joan and Kate Newmann

Train to Derry

A crow beats on the updraft over a scragged hawthorn,
rocked but plunging on. A stick of Paras, bristling with nerves,
coughs and boots forward along the sheugh.
Long after the soldiers have gone, the crows will settle home.

Since Newry, choppers have been battling back and forth
across the track. These trains are overheated, sweat
stings in my underslept eyes; I'd rather the crows' lift and pluck
than to be here, rocked to the quick, driving on Derry.

I often wish, my love, that we were birds, the wide domains
of Ireland at our turn and fall, the world's wind
our natural element—rain, ice, hail or sun our gods,
the tall pines our greenwhip lightning rods.

Tonight there's a horned moon and Venus trailing
low over the Waterside. Tonight let me fold you in my wings,
pray nobody's killed in dark of country or town. We'll settle
the long night in another of our beds, watch what the morning brings.

November in May

Trees in their full weight buffeted by rain,
the plants on the windowsill waterlogged,
a gale pushing down through the gardens
between two tall rows of Georgian houses.

Aerials whip in the wind, birds battered low
go by in fits and starts, the elderflowers are dull
in the sulphurous light, night coming over us
too early, far too early. We stand at the window

cradling cups of tea, trying not to feel cheated.
It was a long winter. God knows, there were days
we hardly thought to survive, and now this wind
battering the glass is breaking our hearts.

Listen, can you hear them breaking? Small sounds,
skitter of claws on slate, mortar tumbling
to a flat roof. A siren grumbles along the canal, muted
and shredded under the weight of the rocking gale.

And still the night to get through, a night of rain falling
while we seek refuge in books, in small, careful sentences
and guarded looks. We walk from room to room avoiding
the bed, talk of the future, the glare of the calendar.

The Geography of Armagh

Somebody's lover is leaving someone home,
a neighbourly duty, a mile or two down
a winding country road.

The orchards are heavy with fruit and dust,
the road unrolling into autumn,
a winding country road.

Somebody's lover at the end of the command wire
watches the headlights burrowing down
a winding country road,

tense as the front wheels bite on a bend
and the car straddles the culvert, then
a winding country road

blown slow, skyward into the harvest moon,
apples hung in the flame tree,
a winding country road

whipcracking aftershock, fountain of earth and fire,
and then the meat and apples settling,
a winding country road

strewn with glass, branch, leaf, flesh, somebody's brother
and his neighbour—the what's left—and
a winding country road

going God alone knows where, a root-flamed ash,
a wire snapped, as somebody's lover takes off
home down a winding country road.

Somewhere

Somewhere there is a simple life,
the snow dredged through a stand of birch,
tracks of a rabbit in the snow, the path
indented on a white page; track
of the wood-cutter, the solitary doctor, the child
trailing homeward to soup, firelight, mother.

I hold this vision in my cupped hands,
a dome of light on the bare table;
there was anguish in that ornament, the shaken snow
made the plastic cottage frail—
I almost remembered a trail home, sitting at home
in firelight, tasting the soup of another life.

Mother, I have been in the cold places I dreamed of
when you were proud of your bright son.
The day the bus went by the back road to Sheremetyevo
I snatched *beriozka* from the rattle of pale trunks,
the word echoing. Tracks of a rabbit in the snow,
my own tracks crossing the trail of childhood.

Never again, my mother, those conversations by firelight.
Somewhere, somewhere there is a simple life.

Red Square

Crack of red silk in the arctic uplights,
yellow of Leningrad in the walls and domes,
oxblood-dull the crenellated walls.

Cresting the rise before the cobbled square,
stone of St. Basil's freighted with bright turbans.
I imagine tank tracks crunching across the setts,

I imagine the steppe wind howling from immense
voids far to the east, but this is a dull night
of afterheat and haze. The square is tired.

It has seen too much of history, too many couples
from solemn places with wedding garlands
for Lenin's tomb, old women burdened

with perhaps-bags, waiting for wind of change,
for a flash of lost gaiety, a surprising question.
The stage is set for a new brute and his programme.

Of Certain Architects, Technicians and Butchers

I am the belly of great armies
I battle the ages in my fear
I am the horror in the newborn child
and the horror in its mother.
Who but I built Ulm cathedral?

I am the great cathedrals of pure thought
I am the frozen wave of the Carpathians
I am the sword that cleaves the knot forever
and the knot itself that closes around the sword.
Who but myself made Alexander weep?

I am the famine when Alexanders weep
I am the sand that built and swallowed Carthage
I am the Hydra drinking Stalin's blood
and the blood that doused the flames of Dresden.
Who but I could darken the air with engines?

I am the engines and the fire at heart
I am the garden and gardener at Treblinka
I am the wolf who howls in Katyn Forest
and the forest itself howling in the wolf.
Who but I would storm the moon?

> I am a forest of great armies
> I am the knot that twists the child
> I am the sword turns in engines
> I am the wolf in the cathedral.

I pace behind mountains, turning the days over;
I wait for the dark star that will shine when I cross.

Nine Views of Uzbekistan 1991

Roses in a bank of snow,
birds of paradise,
leaves in a spring tree—
the eyes of an Uzbek dancing girl.

But wasn't there a curfew?
A flight of masked glances,
a downturning of palms.
A journalistic error, it happens.

Salaam aleikum, not *zdrastvuitye.*
Rachmat, not *spassiba bolshoi.*
This thaws even apparatchiks,
the Union sailing over a reef of vowels.

A police escort fore and aft,
traffic halted at all the junctions.
It is meant for courtesy but, being Irish,
we exchange sceptical glances.

Nasruddin teaching his donkey to read,
Nasruddin as an Asian Sancho Panza—
twenty five centuries since Alexander ruled
this people whose heroes are tyrants and jokers.

Timurlane's teacher has the bigger tomb
but Timurlane's is the name we know;
statues of Lenin everywhere we go,
here and there Nasruddin and his donkey.

Pomegranates, melons, dust and straw
in a market old before Christ was born.
A schoolboy with Ulugbek's eyes greets us
in French. He says he is pleased to see us.

He might be my father's father, he sits on
a spavined donkey as if he might ride to Vienna.
Where from? The eyes unwinking. Ah, Ireland.
Green island. Beyond England, farther than Moscow.

The exquisite mosque has been a museum
since the Revolution, open to all. Last year
the Mullahs paraded, demanding reconsecration.
Ah Jaysus, says one of the lads, I hope you said no.

Béal na mBláth

I have been so long waiting
to say what I must say
the voice of flowers has left me.

Winter is always here.
Stone and water mix in my breath,
a voice divided against itself.

To Gennadi Uranov in the Coming Times

The birches are cooling after a sultry day, and grass
is springing back in the wind of evening. The paths
are dusty, the sound from behind the railings
is the chatter of starlings before dark.

There is the feeling of early in the century, a face at
one of these high windows might have echoed
in Anna Andreevna's heart, pale signal
of love lost, of smoky music, our melancholy art.

She dreamed of a simple life, as our poet dreamed
whose house soaks in the fading light of day;
he turned his face against the century's wall, and she
quietly agreed to play her part.

This man had set his heart on passion's play,
ended in rage that the hero's day was done.
This woman, born to aristocratic ways,
turned to her destiny in a prison's dark.

Walking tonight, I turn their verses over,
sounding the voices of our time,
trying the shape ahead of me in this park
of what is terrible in the days to come.

My heart is muffled like a mourning drum.
There has been so much mourning, wave after wave
climbing the wall of the century, smashing
our courage to splinters of stars

and this is all we have to carry forward:
starlight of prisons, flints & shards of all that is best
in us, a line here, a phrase there, our honour
and glory in fragments over the wide earth.

Tonight I will walk down to the dark Liffey
and stand there until I cannot feel the cold anymore.
I will think of you on the Moskva's embankment
remembering this city, fearing for your own,

and though I am a melancholy pagan
I will pray for an end to this terrible century,
for quiet in your house and in mine, silence
after music for Yeats and Akhmatova.

Garda Waking from a Dream of Language

The rock and tilt of it, the red-wrapped
rump and pelvis of a whore against
the slow beat of my own country feet.
In the railed Square, earth and green
breathing to the right of me, asphalt
to the left, and over it all the unknowing
clouds and above the clouds the loanwords
of stars, jet-trails, hard constellations.

I think of the lies I will be told now if I stop
the young girl with cider in her basket, space
behind her eyes, or the cyclist impatient and testy—
there is no rain, and little traffic, the frame is
light, he's nimble, why should he carry a lamp?
Everyone reaches first for the greasy words,
weightless, investing what's clear with fog and doubt.

The radio on my shoulder at least is
plain, it spits digits, location of units, codes
for crimes and seriousness, names—the slick
electric tracking of the game. Tonight I could trace
answers to questions, right from the foaming nations
who had the first grace of cities to this shop-
window that gives me back my uniform, behind bars.

I think we learned language first beneath clear stars.
Maybe a Persian watchman or a Greek
walking the unquiet nights like this was first
to speak plain against night's unease, the rock

and tilt of it questioned by the red-wrapped
rump and pelvis of a whore, who writes
need and independence into the balance of the night,
who answers me plain and simple from her door.

Speak plain, they told me, say what you mean and
mean what you say. Then it must follow as the night.
The day. Such confidence, father and mother, in your truth.
How would you name these currents, crossed and backed?
All night the roar of holiday jets, lick of quick traffic,
background the chaos logged with such precision in
my ear. Sometimes I ask myself what I'm doing here.
For answer, incline and listen to my feet, resume the beat.

Would I be better, as you dreamed for me,
easing the car now through a soft country lane, home
from a dance with perfume on my hands, thinking
that one, now, is nice, she'd do me grand. Arcadian
dreams to shepherd a language home? There's
a queer word, one that'd lose a sergeant. I choose,
and they won't understand me, in spite of all,
the script of street and city, this hard full stop.

Kilmainham Gaol, Dublin, Easter 1991

Roadies in ponytails stringing lights and cables,
a beer can popped in the corner, echo of sound check.
Outside in the filling yard, hum of expectation.

We pour through the narrow gate under the gallows hook
in twos and threes, becoming an audience.
Before the lights go down we examine each other shyly.

The singer surveys his audience, heat rising
to the tricolour and Plough overhead.
As the first words of Galvin's lament climb to invoke
James Connolly's ghost, we are joined by the dead.

I say this as calmly as I can. The gaunt dead
crowded the catwalks, shirtsleeved, disbelieving.
The guards had long since vanished, but these
looked down on us, their faces pale.

I saw men there who had never made their peace,
men who had failed these many years to accept their fate,
still stunned by gunfire, wounds, fear for their families;
paralysed until now by the long volleys of May so long ago.

I think that we all felt it, their doubt and their new fear,
the emblems so familiar, the setting, our upturned faces,
so unreal. Only the dignity of the singer's art
had power to release them. I felt it, I say this calmly.

I saw them leave, in twos and threes, as the song ended.
I do not know that there is a heaven but I saw their souls
fan upward like leaves from a dry book, sped out into the night
by volleys of applause; sped out, I hope, into some light at last.

I do not know that I will ever be the same again.
That soft-footed gathering of the dead into their peace
was like something out of a book. In Kilmainham Gaol
I saw this. I felt this. I say this as calmly and as lovingly as I can.

for Frank Harte

Seven Versions of Loss Eternal

1

Imagine the salt caking an evening sand-rose,
a steep dune sprawling towards the infinite,
a lone traveller trying hard not to fall—
lost in the sands, hallucinating trinities—
imagine his thirst for reconciling fountains,
for the three jets made one in the sun's blind strobe,
for the three paths rounding to where she waits.

2

Green cracked linoleum, the oak door shredding
wind and rain-dark into spindrift,
dust and hot paint behind him, the day's labour
already lost in a settling of files. Hand on his collar
he pauses a moment, irresolute, almost lost
but she is not there, never will be again. A paper clip
clicks against change in his pocket, and here's his bus.

3

What is must be like from space, imagine,
the child's nightmare downwardness, the globe
blue, green and watered, the great mountains
scored like ribs across a carcase, cities
winking on and off, deltas a great scrawl
of mud and silt on the blue-green flush of silk—
to be there and never to go down again.

4

The projector ticks as it cools, metal and glass
going lifeless with electricity shut off. His hand
spins with the deadweight of the rewind arms,
his mind as vacant as the cinema far below.
In the tang of hot celluloid he hesitates to think
of where he might go now there is nowhere to go,
a man becoming a shadow of himself.

5

Imagine the great Atlantic waves, rearing to freeze
far over him—embattled and stubborn, raw from spray
and cold and drenching, the radio gone, the stars unseen
for days now, unable for even a moment to go below;
a rag of topsail's enough to drive him on, harder and deeper
by the minute, as long as his wrists hold out.
Her blue handkerchief wound around his watchstrap.

6

Salt on the butcher block of beech, he leans hard
on his circling hands, the brush scouring the work away
in the blue light from the window. He has learned
not to breathe too deeply in this quiet time, never
to look at his hands until he has scrubbed them clean.
He clicks off the light with his back to the street,
the most terrifying moment of his day.

7

Imagine your whole day is a search for a missing sign—
you scan rivers of paper, faces drifted in the streets,
magazine illustrations, cinema posters, the blank
windows of schools, offices, factories. You listen
to bus tyres in the rain, at night you sneak sudden glances
at clouds ripping past the stars. Nothing.
An irregular contraction in the chest. Nothing.

A Neighbour of Ours

The lift of a linnet's wing was all he asked,
with the fog a light gold over the brewery and
the bells tumbling over sweet Blackpool
from the North Chapel, Shandon, the Assumption,
to be standing on Richmond Hill
and the pale sun shining,
a day in October, the air clear in his head.

Nothing out of the ordinary, a simple perfect moment;
the lift of a linnet's wing was all he asked for, and got.

for Gerry Murphy

The Life I Live Now

I throw my head back in the street,
in the hum of evening traffic
on the black rainslick street.
I regard the stars without feeling.

As if they were raindrops in a web,

as if they were phrases in an electric
frame, crystals that might arc into
my skull like perfect diminutives—
to die in my heart, where you have died.

A Man is Standing on a White Beach, Knowing that He Must Die

It rolls on the crisp white shore,
folds in upon itself and comes to rest
back in the darkness from the lamplight pool,
all that I ever cared for in this life.

It might be a poem, the language salt with life,
teasing the memory of Sunday by a pool,
or it might be your words, first laboured, then at ease,
recalled while we watch this unfamiliar shore.

Northing is ever simple on this shore—
here where the page is margin to a life—
no more than light that gathers in a pool
hungry to taste a sea that cannot rest.

Whatever, I know I never will have rest
until the isolated moments pool
and we stand out to speak of simple life,
the dead words abandoned on the shore.

What Lives We Lead

I woke from dreams of gunfire to the sound of sirens,
crossing my own footsteps at a remove in time.

Without leaving my bed, suddenly I am there.

So many ambush points in a known place,
the precise angle where two walls meet,
the exact shadow cast by a hanging sign.
He was there in the plane of light from the great window,
my younger self, that dust-devil,
turning forever angrily on himself.

Brewery men dropping barrels onto a stuffed sack,
the dull percussive thuds, the cheerful obscenities
and the half-humorous eyes, angling from under caps—
I must have looked odd, stopping suddenly as if struck.

So many years ago, and the pain again so piercing.
What lives we lead, after all!

Trial by Existence

I am the rimlight electric child
aureate against the indigo of night;
I am the child of love made in the dark
by bodies urgent to touch what does not die.

I am the ghostchild of the timelines
in the air outside your window,
riding the updraft like a leaf.
I am as blue and bright as sudden grief.

With your companion you work the hidden light,
each gesture, each caress easing the husk open
until bodies break from flesh,
until there is breath only,
climbing to fuse in breath, and light
stabs in the dark like a landing beacon.

I am the child of light from far-off stars,
sucked from a clean run through space
down through the whirlpool of raw need,
the cry of the womb for fullness, a charm against death.

I am the spark to leap the gap, I am the gap that I must cross.
When the air is thick with passion I lean on your lungs,
when you burn and reach out it is I who burn,
it is towards me that you forever reach.

I am the child eager for life, listen to me,
I am a bitter death where love is not.
I am a star in daytime and good health
where the room rocks in the pitch of hard-won love.

The Inquisitor Considers the Daughters of Eve

Before they are born I love their unmoving silence,
but when the rot sets in and breath draws life
from silence and their eyes open, it all starts up—
the long flux of arrogance and decay.

Their flesh is enchanted by a word;
flesh, womanjuice, seed and clay
reduced in a sweaty sac. Choice is their word
for what they lack, chosen obedience to the will of God.

Death is my enemy and choice is death's word.
When I hear it whispered in my ear at night I know
the Devil walks, and wake to sweat and pray—
we were not made to choose but to obey.

They spin and dip like insects over the festering earth,
liars and witches who would burn for shame
if they heard God's word on them, if they knew the Word
as I do, who am sent among them with a sword of fire.

All day in the city there is murmuring against me.
The women say I corrupt the young, they say my photographs
and specimens are evil, they say their children lie awake
rigid with fear because of me, because of my witness.

Let their children gag on truth: the only beauty is unborn.
There is no innocence in the quick, let them burn
in their beds, let them do the Will from fear
if from nothing else. My father taught me there is nothing else.

I Remember a Night in the Long Valley

There we were with the light
pouring out of us onto
the round and famous table.
Even Humphrey was laughing,

calling Time! Time!
like a barman in a fable.
In the wind off the clock
the red-eyed drinkers turned

half-faces towards us:
the fang and the smile,
benediction and curse.
The bells boomed

in my head, the familiar
sliding slow into the strange.
Somebody kissed my ear.
The spittle after—sticky, cold.

The Woman Who Was an Eagle

She is a voice through which stone extends an empire.
She is a silence deeper than my most vertiginous fall
into fear. She'd stop me now with one swift look. Her
dreaming is redolent of the sea at nightfall, pulsing salt.

When she'd come from the garden, green would come with her.
I have seen her at dusk become luminous in an owl's call
of salutation. Beads burn in the stream of her speech. Where
she'd walk I would range behind her, scarcely daring talk.

Mountain, moorland, where I am blind she sees entire.
Lands I tremble at she has claimed, traversed, survived. And all
enriches her. She has never looked for comfort. Her heart
is a well, sunk in rich earth and rock, down which I fall.

She has placed on my tongue salt of forgetting, I will not forget.
I bite back my voice in the city streets, finding no place to speak
        her proper name.

She Says

Empty yourself,
red wine wells to the lip

It is time now,
and already too late

Forget me,
I am always with you.

Drowned in wine and forgetfulness
breathe easy, loose your grip,

I call all things to dance with me
in the ripening of time.

A Slow Poem

I place my finger with great care
on the sleeping magnificent body of my beloved.
The room is quiet and huge, the air still, so still
I hear dustmotes falling like leaves on the counterpane.

I stop my breathing and she fills me up
with swell of breath, the rise and fall of tides
so quiet and silver there, I am carried up and out of touch;

and she is far below me, curled into me,
her skin sufficient boundary, her dreams and trouble stilled.
Her troubles become diamond in my chest, I tip and balance

here beneath the ceiling, full of airy, thoughtful love, then fall
as slowly as leaves falling on a field,
until I settle there beside her, breathing her breath.

The Backward Look

Summer was standing in the high corn, each stem
stiff with minerals, the seed-husks packed with bread.

You breasted feathered heads, wading towards me, your eyes
blazing, your palms like rudders trailing and a swift

dropped suddenly out of the blue, tracing a perfect arc,
a flash of compact muscle bursting past.

And still you came on, and still I see you wading,
your brown bare feet scuffing the dust,

with each pace nearer as the picture recedes and you are framed
by the long hill that rises up behind you

in willowherb, heather, gorse and ash. Draw close, the fire
is glowing in the hearth, nest your dark head here on my shoulder

and see what I see: high summer, the life that is to be,
me like a scarecrow planted there, heart packed

with straw and joy and promise, a swift stitching the compact
that brings you on. Rain beats on the window, a gust

rattles the chimney-pots but the fire's well set, and bread
is cooling in the kitchen. Our kitchen. Our first summer. This life.

The Second Fortune

Between what is and what is not
we walked, the Huntress loosed a shot.

Before and after, we were there—
the arrow pierced but singing air.

That, my love, was quite an art,
to be together and apart

yet we, transparent, without fear—
what were we but singing air?

On Knockmealdown

And, you ask, is there a song
naming this land laid low beneath?

Only this turbulent wind, driving from
here down through the oceanic trees.

The Edge

In a million mites of crystal
the beach dreams fusing to glass.

The high sun yearns for the blue
forgetfulness of the blue sea.

Miro's House for Lovers

My love, he writes, I have found us a house,
a farmhouse in Catalonia, such a house
as would shelter dreaming lovers.

There is a tree in the garden, rooted
in the void, shod in white enamel against goats.
It has leaves like the feathers of wet crows.

The ground floor was a stable once,
the top floor a granary. The windows are small,
neat against wind and sun.

There is a lean-to with an old hooped wagon,
a cistern for drawing water, a columbarium,
and oh, the red, red earth of the garden!

Listen to me, the light is exactly right.
The letter of all beginnings could root in that light
under a sky so blue the midday moon shines through.

A Charm on the Night of Your Birthday

I light the sky above our bed for you
with seven stars of gold, ploughing
the deep for you—and that's not so hard
when you are the sea.

I rock in my ribs here in your absence,
my heart like a diesel thudding away
and you at the helm, friend and guide
steering through for me.

I'll sleep now, soon, under seven stars,
the plough in the night dipping towards you,
your ghost on deck above holding our course,
your bones asleep in me.

My blue pillow is wrapped in your shirt
and my head is bedded in the scent of your hair;
I'll make your hair a sail to carry me
from here to over there.

Western

A painted pony floats in tall grass,
rises and plunges with
all the time in the world.

The grasses are dryheaded, flecky with dust
they wheel around him in great arcs
under billows of wind.

The day's weight goes down in his plunge,
the air heaves with his roll of shoulder.
Telescope in on the seedflecked hock, his unwinking eye.

The bridle is plaited rope. A wishbone of sweat
on back and flanks where the rider was.
She is floating now through the tall grass,

the lark and the swift see her bent back
and the cracked stalk milks her step and instep.
The wind dips, tips my scent into her face.

She holds the hunting-blade low in her fist,
the grasses brush at her breasts and belly,
her hunter's cheekbone, striped with desire.

A red sun glares from the Dublin mountains,
I slip into a downdraft, dropping east from the ridge.

The Odds

Fan of black hair against the pillow,
we have been here before.

What light there is
gathers into her star pupils.

She is thinking of sandwaves
drifted against sunset,
and he is thinking of rain
scudding through grasses
against the wall of her house.

Night beats on the window.
Will it be this time?
Neither can tell.
For now there is sand
against rain, chance
against destiny.

The nerve of risk
flicking against adultery.

Enchanted, she murmurs,
testing the word on his face,
I am *enchanted*.

The Astronomer of Love

Out there, a galaxy
curls in upon itself,
hung
in the sparkling bowl of night—

I am testing this when
between breath and breath
I flick sideways
and find you fragile in your flight.

Light in the cheekbones
breaking through,
light in the sockets
beneath clamped lids,

a bronze warrior
fit for
the shock of steel on bone,
but plunging on

into the heart of night,
ice plumes fanning wide
into the wake of your wild rise;

far from the home planet,
aimed at the world out there,
the ice becoming silver
in your hair.

Between breath and breath I brush
a kiss upon your cheek.
You open direct from sleep,
a nebula whirling in each fabulous eye.

Me, John Wayne & the Delights of Lust

Sometimes I wake and find you
so trustingly curled against me
I forget to breathe.
The impulse toward sentiment
irresistible, I back away down the ladder
with that aw-shucks John Wayne face on
and go to make tea,
counting my blessings as diligently
as the child I was would tell his rosaries
before he got sense.

I get sense, returning with the heavy tray,
when you stir, crack an eye open and ask
"Oh love, what kind of a morning is it . . ?"
Nothing in this world better than
that moment when, me laid up alongside
and the waves ebbing towards the planted palm
by the window, you stretch to your full length
and light two cigarettes, fixing me with a grin,
an out-of-focus, complicit, quizzical look.
John Wayne to hell, I think, and phone in sick.

Driver

Rain beats on the windshield as she drives,
rain of the southern winter under the Cross.
Rain slicks from the tyres as she takes curves
one after the other in slow motion.

The white line unpeels before her eyes,
an envelope thumbed open, the letter showing through.
She leans into the next curve, and the next,
impatient to read the signature, to read *love*...

The rain is everywhere tonight, even
the radio plays Rainy Night in Georgia;
it can be like that when you are caught, the world
rounding to a closed set of curves.

Absolute concentration empties her out
into the night, her hands on the wheel
are light but firm, as if gripping his shoulders
—which slowly, imperceptibly, she is.

A letter is waiting for her at journey's end;
she smiles, shifting down to third,
smiles and sobers to think what lies behind cliché,
hearing what beats on the windshield as his voice.

Something hypnotic in the long procession of curves,
the low hum of tyre-grooves in light rain,
sets her to settle back easy in her heart,
to wind the whole journey into a song of his name.

for M. B.

Under Mercury

My blood and my brain are bound to his rule,
that trickster and lightfoot, the male thief
who watched over my birth.

Sometimes a solid earthflush fills my veins—
as now, watching your feet flick out,
inviting the plunge.
And I think that I could live like this
but it never quite works out.

Sooner or later we both come and then it's
me for the gate of disappearances,
the blue silence, love's long dark.

Valley Dream

There is a valley crested with broad pine,
threaded with rivers and willow, opening
westward to the sea. I saw us there last night
on a low ridge, as the sun was going down.

Martin, swift or swallow, it wasn't clear
what the birds were, flickering on the staves
the powerlines made stepping out across the valley.
They stitched and unpicked the twilight, a song of air.

You sighed, and my breathing settled; stretched,
and a great ease flowed through my limbs.
You turned, and splinters of late sunlight
glanced from your eyes, cut razor-sharp through mine.

She Buckles in Her Sleep

Close now, the hurt that has you hurt yourself.

I hear it trickle over the cut edge in your sleep,
the drain of meaning, trust, all that we have
to sing back the dark, the spirit's poverty.

Curl in my arms and sigh, and settle here.
I am no saint or saviour, and I am your grief
too often, though I would not be.

Shelter, shelter and kindness, this embrace
and this belief: we are nearing the still centre
where love is again possible, and strange, and rich.

White Stone Promises

If on a dark night after searching
until my mind is nearly gone from me
I bring you your mother Akhmatova
with her pale hands turned young again
to soothe the unquiet from your face,
what will you do for me?

I ask three things only:

A night and a day in the dark
of your eyes without sleep,

The stone that Fearbhlaidh had from Cearbhall
with the white of your breast in it,

Never to leave my dreaming
without saying where you may be found.

Crossing the Shannon in broad sunlight
I ask these things of you.
You shall have what you need
while there is breath in me.

First Lesson

Space within and space without
I made a body with a shout.
You flowed around me into trees
and soothed me with song.

Sun within and sun without,
revolving I called up a drought.
My dry breath scorched the trees,
you fled into a thread of water.

Space within and sun without
I blessed the world with a strong shout.
A green breeze revived the trees
and you came back to flow inside me.

Cryptic tales are quickly told
and hold the mind has wit to hold them.
Only experts of the heart
will understand your gift, my art.

Her Hawk, Her Messenger

This also, to be
spreadeagled on a tossed bed
scream of hawk in the high pines
resin on the air, unmerciful light
on the whitewashed wall
noon, not her hour
so where does this come from
again and again
the crescent axeblade sighing through skin
the bone spraying out in white chips
blood spraying out after bone
through the ribs over and over
the same blow forever and ever
again and again
spreadeagled on a tossed bed
my head on your dress
lead in ankle and wrist
racked on the ironframe bed
again and again
resin on the air, and blood
scream of a hawk
the axe from behind through the ribs
over the heart
and the heart feeling nothing, nothing
forever, again and again.

Trespasser

Blood on her thighs from the long climb
through waist-high thorns from the sea.
Dust filming the blood, killing
reflection. Calmly she rolls her palms
in the paste, blunts highlights from her brow.

Dust on the olive as she leans her cheek
against rough, nightsilvered bark.
Somewhere ahead, a charcoal fire
spits and hangs heavy on the resiny air
smoke and fat of a crackling rabbit.

Now she is moving like a gust of night,
Longlegged, slow, upwind of the hunter.
She makes her eyes knife-slits.
Her pupils darken, flint-shards.
Darts fixed on the nape of his neck.

His back to the gully and the moon,
his lungs full of thyme, myrtle,
smoke of the fire and fat,
he leans back, smug and content.
Lights a last cigarette before turning in.

Kato Zakros

It is called the Gorge of the Dead.
The burial caves are punched in yellow rock,
spiked by a jewelled fist, an invader's.

Sand underfoot, and dust, everything clear, precise.
Your sandaled foot falls there, and there, and there—
the mesmeric clarity of rock and asphodel,

the exact blue of the scarf that binds your hair.
You carry a bent stick as if it were a bow,
and flare at the edges, light coming out of you.

You have the hunter's steady lope, ready to go
anywhere, risk anything on instinct
and I need water, I need courage, I need rest.

I follow the blue flag and your hair,
your head a bright bird darting the gorge
stooping now, and now, and now.

Potsherds, a fragment of rim, a handle-stump—
I stoop to pick them up, sun high between walls
and my head hard in the heat.

I rattle my talismans, hoping to make you turn,
greasing the potter's thumbprint with my own.
How clear it all is, not a puff of air

until you punch my lungs with a look.
Hearts leap, I know, I felt it, I still feel it
here in the dark, tracking you through sunlight.

Voice in an Airport

Out of so many voices, one.
Out of the electric frame,
a single crystal ringing
on and on in empty halls.

For my ear only, as the whole
departure lounge is for me
only. Roar at the end of
the runway, four exhausts
flaming up into the black.

To speak again we will need wire
and fibre optic, satellite ticking
in the blue cold overhead—
never again a world coiled in a look,
pulse breathing crystal into pulse.

Corridor Vision, Nuremore Hotel

Behind her eyes
that fugitive thing,
the lock on what is real.

The sweet note, the pain
and what is beyond pain
in a hitch of shoulder, turn
or tuck of wrist.

She reaches to touch my face and I
am completely undone.

Walking Shoes

I think of the day we parted and how my heart turned;
you were lacing on walking shoes, shoes for your
winter, shoes for walking away from sunlight,
the room darkening as you straightened & looked down.

Later, the cab ticking out towards the airport.
The checking of documents, practical affairs,
and then the tannoy calls to separate terminals,
panic in look and kiss, departure's business.

You write that yellow leaves are piled in drifts
near the footbridge where you walk to compose yourself.
I imagine them sticking to your shoes, I imagine rain,
walking all day myself against the grain.

Mirror

Silence an ocean, as air is, and we
but small things moving
in a strong light, the last days
of winter held us fast.

There was a crisp perfection
in the black grass, in the twigs
laid underfoot, the sweep
of water coasting the path.

No wind on those days,
our breath as we walked
trailed streamers in and out
between the birches.

Each word steps firmly out
and stands in time's gaze.
I set these things down in silence,
fire for the ice of our old age.

Quiet

What moves hugely in the garden after dark
is no concern of ours, my love. Be still.

Here we contend with demons of the hearth,
with quiet in our household we may venture out.

You Made Your Hair a Sail to Carry Me

Mackerel were turning in slow rolls under the keel,
as we coasted out the wind brought wood- and turf-smoke
from bungalows settling for the summer night.
Along the horizon clouds were turning bright.

Away from landfall, away into the west
we bent under sail, the silence of work coming over us
as the stars came gleaming out. A wave came on abaft
and lifted us, so that the rudder gleamed in air

before we settled, skipping the shock, into a north-running trough.
The long rhythm of it all, the sea, the night, the journey,
what your face said when the danger had passed,
and what your hand said tilting my face to the sky,
is what endures now of the whole year's run.

Eclipse

She lifts her skirt above her head
and a black disc hangs in heaven;

her chin is over her shoulder & her eyes
probe deep into the heft of space.

Silent, and almost without breathing
we watch the spray from her flung hair

hang shocked and still. Ships crawl on the sea,
sailors ashore in the loud bars are unsettled.

We light a candle on the windowsill
for a thread of light from here to over there,

Arachne's line, bent silver with her tears,
child of the zodiac banished into dark.

And slowly our mother lets her skirt fall,
her wrist leads heavy cloth in a downward arc

drawing the black bull forward;
we know that she cannot afford to miss.

Memory packed in his meaty neck,
all that is blood and smoke and pain of pride
in the wide, arrogant sweep of his horns,
the knot of history muscular in his shoulder.

In the steep galleries of shade and fear,
stars flare as the steel drives home.

I cup Arachne's breast, tilt your bright face
to the moon and me, you kiss me for charm

and promise, your legs float up around my waist
and I jet deep and sure in your womb.

The candleflame gutters in a wind from space,
tilts left and right, then grips. Downstairs

the sailors are singing and at peace; the air
is kind, no one at sea tonight will come to harm.

for PM on her birthday, 25 vi 92

Taverna on the Beach

Pomegranate thumbed open to reveal generations,
apple split to its white heart of flesh.
Ultramarine waters lap at stone,
lacing our days of light with drift of salt.
All night we cry and laugh and you
taste ash of apple on my skin—
delighting in apple, pomegranate, light and salt.

Deep in your veins you carry light of salt,
testing the fruit against dryness under skin,
and unexpected urgencies push through,
laughter the remedy for the deep fault
under the streets, the reek of ancient stone.
All that the heart and mind can learn from flesh
piled in a rampart against the dead generations.

Watcher

With a head hard since time began
I watch the harvests come and go,
refusing to choose between the trees and men,
watching the signatures they make
spark in the summer haze.
I endure this only because I must.

Water draining through the ground beneath me,
limestone pavement crazed in the sun.
St. John's Wort sprouts from the fissures,
blossom and dust straggled in my hair.
The downslope sweating into streams.
Time is the dry leaf of my attention.

Sometimes I see what might be ships from home,
arcing across the ache, then winking out.
It has been a long station
and still I am unmoved.
At night I stare into the hub of galaxies,
their ponderous wheeling hurts my head.

The Old Man

An old man sits at a crossroads in the dust.
He owns herds and diamonds,
mines running deep underground,
cattle numerous as leaves on the dust in autumn.
All day the sun of the world beats on his head.
All day he sits in the light but sees nothing;
because he is blind, because he is suffocating in rage.

He lashes with the sjambok
at anyone who brings him water
at anyone who brings him words
at anyone who says
"Lay down the burden of your cares old man,
we are younger than you and we are many,
we will take up your cares and make them our own".

Oh many young men and women say to him
"Lay down the burden of your cares old man,
and the light of the world will not be harsh,
the call of the children in their hunger will not be sharp,
there will be meat and diamonds, water and milk
for you and your children's children and
for us and our childrens' children."

An old man sits at a crossroads in thick dust,
he is blind because he is sitting in his own shadow.

Let him unpick this riddle and we will take him by the hand.
When he unpicks this riddle, he will get up and walk away.

The High Salt Graveyard

The wind makes pebbles clip
the plastic wreath-case. Pines
behind me skip and toss,
a dry creaking without cease.

I come to think on his arrested flight.
I come to let the wind blow through me.

The Match Down the Park

Tom Knott comes bulling out, his shoulder down
bringing weight to bear on the sliothar dropping
from his hand. The crack of ash on leather echoes
the length of the Park.

Like a new evening star, the ball
climbs the November air, a clean
white flash in the cold and cloud.

All of the faces around me turn
like plates to the sky, tracking the rising arc.
Over the halfway line now, and dropping into
a clash of hurleys, forward shouldering back.

Our jerseys are brighter than theirs
in this eerie light, the black and amber
fanning out into a line, a berserk charge.

My face is jammed through the flat bars
of the gate, the goalposts make me dizzy
leaning back to look up. The goalie is jittery,
the chocolate melts in my fist, I hear myself

howling from a great distance
Come on Piarsaigh, come on, face up, face up . . .
Sound stops in a smell of mud and oranges.

I can feel the weight of them bearing down on goal,
I can't see, Mr Connery is roaring and Johnny Parker,
I bet even my Dad is roaring, back there in the crowd
but I can't leave the gate to go see, I can't—

a high ball, a real high one, oh God
higher than the moon over the fence towards Blackrock,
it's dropping in, they're up for it, Pat Kelleher's fist

closes on leather, knuckles suddenly badged with blood
in the overhead clash; he steadies, digs in his heel,
he turns, shoots from the 21—
the whole field explodes in my face.

A goal! A goal! Their keeper stretched across his line,
his mouth filled with mud, the sliothar feet from my face,
a white bullet bulging the net.

Everything stops.

A ship comes gliding on the high tide, her hull
floating through the elms over the rust-red stand.
A man on the flying-bridge looks down on us.

I race back to my father, threading the crowd,
watching for heavy boots, neck twisting back
to the net still bulging, the ship still coming on,
the green flag stabbed aloft, the final whistle.

Sixpence today for the bikeminder under his elm.
Men in dark overcoats greeting my Dad
Well done Bert, ye deserved it. And
A great game, haw? Ah dear God what a goal!

I'm introduced as the eldest fella. *Great man yourself.*
Men anxious to be home, plucking at bikes, pushing away.
The slope to the river, the freighter drawing upstream.

And then the long, slow pedal home,
weaving between the cars on Centre Park Road,
leaning back into the cradle of his arms.

That was some goal, wasn't it Dad?
It was indeed, it was. His breath warm on my neck;
a wave for the man on Dunlop's gate,
we'll pass the ship tied up near City Hall.

He's a knacky hurler, Pat Kelleher.
        He is Dad, ah jay he is.
By God, that was the way to win.
        It was, Dad, it was.

for Na Piarsaigh on their fiftieth anniversary

Skull of a Curlew

Skull of a curlew full of stars,
my mouth on fire with black, unspeakable bees.
Light on the lime boles, bleached and bare,
my gorge rising, crammed with blackfurred bees.

Clay of the orchard on my cheek,
cheeks puffed like wind on a map's margin.
Dust in each lungful of cold air,
lips burned on the inside by black bees.

> I wait for the moon to rise me
> I pray to the midnight ant
> I clutch at fistfuls of wet grass
> I hammer the earth with bare heels.

Skull of a curlew full of stars,
night sky dredged with the eyes of bees.
Black fire around each star,
I swallow fear in mouthfuls of fur and wing.

Skull of a curlew full of stars,
the great hive of heaven heavy around me.
I spit out bees and black anger,
mouth of a curlew, fountain of quiet stars.

From the Sirian Agronomist's Report

So we buried the secret in a grain of sand
and left them to go fork-legged at it,
inventing plough and husbandry to turn
their chosen portion of the crust.

Aeons watched mountains fold over over into dust.
Hedged armies manoeuvred and clashed,
stoop-bellied ships worked out the warp and weft
until cartographers with their black arts
trammelled the globe to a version of itself.

In the black book of forgetting
we taught them the war of mind and matter;
in the green of the jungles we laid clue in fly and spider,
we stitched their skies with the coded flight of birds,
traced rune and alphabet in crests of the sea.

Came a time when their telemetry stabbed crisp and stiff
to the far reaches where our ships held
back and barely out of view.
We thought they had turned the trick inside itself,
by breath and thought and light had found it out.

Still we held off, their jewelled hives winking
a code they neither read nor founded.
The women who knew us we held, counselled and caught.
They turned and they turn in our webs and we leave them
to go as they please, to speak or to hold their peace.

Sometimes we flash in their skies or we glow in the corn,
when the light at evening falls just so on a deserted street,

or a lover is cheered to see death dared in a look,
redemption in silence—that is us too, and more—

as the painter knew, who saw angels on the stairs
when our envoys grew careless or vain.
He caught a formula once in a fragment of conversation,
wrote it down plain. Much good it did them, they hear and forget.
Their own worst enemies, our future and our fear.

Rosa Mundi

April, a day off school. Indulged, bored, hungry for something new.
The road bends below Driscoll's and I see her coming clear,
laden with shopping bags, eyes bright in the full flow of talk.

I've been signalling Collins Barracks on the hill across Blackpool,
morse book open on the window-sill, weighted with a cup.
Nobody answering no matter how I flash
"Help, I am being held prisoner . . ."

It sets in early, disillusion with the State, its idle soldiers.
Flash of her eyes as she greets Peg Twomey now. I scamper upstairs,
hook the bevelled mirror back in place. From the bedroom window

I see her reach the gate.

How he'd tumble downstairs, crash through the front door, taking
    the garden steps
two, three at a time. Up close, the strain on her face.
Tufnell Park years later, the fireflash of news in my face. The
    silence after.

Grooves in her fingers, released from the heavy bags, the rings—
wedding, engagement, eternity—clicking against his nails.
Remembering suddenly when she smiles that he is meant to be sick.

Slowly, backwards, up the steps, her scraps of thought and talk as
    she fought
For breath. Who she'd met and who had died, who was sick and
    who had
a new child, news from a world she waded in, hip-deep in currents
    of talk.

A spoon for each of us and a spoon for the pot, not forgetting to
scald the pot.
What a span of such days unreeling now, my eye on them both,
reaching
down through the haze to bring them back: herself and her son,

my mother and me.

Dust everywhere when they broke the news, my friends, these
sudden strangers.
Dust of the Underground on my lips, dust on their newpainted
window, dust
on the leaves outside, in the heavy air banked high over London town.

I stared down at their gate, a vacuum in my chest, hands clenching
& unclenching.
So fluent the words, so treacherous the comfort.
Old enough to know I had failed her,
too young to know what in, too greedy for life, really, to have cared
enough.

This is the ring I conjure for them, the stage for their dance.
For a child to live, his mother must die. For a man to die, his
mother must live.
Here on the brink of forty, close to midnight, I conjure them all—

my brothers and sisters, my mother and father, my neighbours and
friends,
the most absolute strangers of my life, my heart's companions.
Nothing
is ever lost that has shone light on simple things.

No child is without a mother, no father can lose his son,
no mother is unregarded, no sister can fail to learn,
no brother escapes unwounded, no friend can salve the burn.

The road bends out into the drunken heft of space and nothing
        can be lost.
Not her life's sacrifice, not our unquenched and stubborn love,
not that child's faith in light flashing from mirrors, or her faith in

the human flow of talk. The human flow of talk is all we have.
        Who we've met
and who is sick, who's had a child, who's lost a job. Her eyes flash,
he scampers upstairs, rushes downstairs, taking the steps two at a time,

feeding his heart's hunger for life and life only. The mask of strain
        on her face,
the ritual of the teapot, hesitant access of heartbreak and knowledge.
I would these words could soothe the pain from her fingers,
conjure now and forever her patient grace.

ACKNOWLEDGEMENTS

THE ORDINARY HOUSE OF LOVE (Salmon Publishing, Galway, 1991)
Ambit, The Cork Review, Cyphers, Disarm, Dundalk Poetry Anthology, Fortnight, The Great Book of Ireland / Leabhar Mór na hÉireann, Hill Field, The Irish Times, Living Landscape Anthology, New Irish Writing (The Sunday Tribune), 1990 (USA), *Orbis, Poetry Ireland Review, Poetry Nottingham, Poets for Africa, Quarryman, Rebel, Salmon, Stet, Theatre Ireland, Thistledown (Poems for UNICEF), Triskel Poets 2.*

A number of these poems appeared in a broadsheet, *Triskel Poets 1,* with Thomas McCarthy. A further selection appeared in the broadsheet *Words...Pictures,* with illustrations by Val Bogan. 'At The Lubyanka', 'But This is Most Irregular', 'In The Metro, Moscow' and 'The Thaw' were first published as *Moscow Quartet* (Dublin, The Sweatshop Press, 1989). A number of these poems were broadcast on RTÉ Radio, on BBC Northern Ireland and on Denmarks Radio.

ROSA MUNDI (Salmon Publishing, Galway, 1995)
Cyphers, Poetry Ireland Review, Exposure, The Irish Times, Poetry (Chicago), *Southern Plains Review* (USA), *Southern Review* (USA), *The Ripening of Time, Trinity Poetry Broadsheet, Undr* and *Windows.*

Some of these poems, or versions of them, were broadcast on BBC Radio 4, BBC Radio Ulster, RTÉ Radio 1 and Radio 2.

'Nine Views of Uzbekhistan' first appeared as a pamphlet from The Harkin Press, Dublin 1992. 'The Match Down The Park' was commissioned by Na Piarsaigh Hurling and Football Club (Cork) to mark their fiftieth anniversary. 'To Gennadi Uranov in The Coming Time' won the Poetry Prize at Listowel in 1992. 'The Geography of Armagh' was a prize-winner in the British National Poetry Competition 1992.

Printed in the United Kingdom
by Lightning Source UK Ltd.
128438UK00001B/421-531/P